WHAT HAPPENED TO THE CHURCH?

KEMI ADESOLA

CONTENTS

FOREWORD

'I will build my church the gates of hell shall not prevail against it'-Jesus of Nazareth.

The church has changed, the church is changing, the people inside the church has changed.

Change is happening everywhere; the church should not be an exception because changes affect everything and everybody.
    Church finance and donation pattern is changing, messages attendance outreach system fellowship communications strategies and love languages have changed.

The moral standard and values we support and uphold in the church for centuries has also been affected.

The landscape of Christianity has been altered radically over the decades and we are all left to manage the changes.
    While some Christians are expecting a fantastic result from the church and God even when this change is not prop-

erly executed or inspired by Him others are carrying the huge responsibility of coping with the effects of bad changes and corrupting influence on the church system.

Other groups are sitting on the fence or completely deserted the church playing the proverbial 'prodigal son'.

From the days of one version of the holy bible to over 300 versions and more on the way Christian's have a responsibility to keep the church and the world to the unchanging standard of God's words

God remains unchanged forever but His systems changes concerning different dispensations to allow us to move close to Him.

COMMON PERCEPTIONS OF CHURCH

The Greek name for the church is Eklesia which means – 'The called out'

The bible says' He has called us out of darkness into His marvelous light.

The church is a place for transformation. No one can access the secret of God until they are transformed and the agent of transformation is the word of God - Rhema

Which transforms the soul and the outlook to life.

The bible is full of transformed people that were called out of an old life into a new assignment for God. Jacob, Joseph and Moses were all transformed by their experiences and encounters with God.

Jacob was transformed after his encounter with God in a dream Joseph in prison and Moses by the burning bush.

Even Jesus Christ went through the process at the river Jordan before he commenced his ministry.

Salvation comes through the transformation of the human spirit soul but to transform the soul is more complicated because it involves waiting maturing and becoming like Christ who came to save and mould us to the image of the father.

Many have received mixed messages about what the church is about.

The church is open to anybody but only those who accepts the call to discipleship wilfully and to those who understand their calling to sainthood.

Some sections of the community were asked to give what their perception of what a church should be, and the responses were varied, though most of them were similar, especially in the area of acceptance. We all want to be accepted and feel welcome everywhere we go.

I agree with them that the atmosphere of the church is very important to welcome everybody into the house of God , the attitude of leaders is also relevant to this acceptance culture though there is that temptation to build a Christian nest and keep to our self, keeping the outside world away.

Even the disciples of Jesus Christ displayed this 'nesting' attitude when children came to the lord.

He asked them to allow the young ones to come ' for theirs is the kingdom of God'.

In other words, the church belongs to Jesus and the pattern of implementing every church must come from Him through prayer and the counsel of the holy spirit.

CHURCH AND HUMAN CULTURE

Sociology has taught us that culture shapes us and we are socialised by different agents of the society. We have six continents and hundreds of countries countless tribes and languages.

Even the bible has been translated into many languages because scholars realised the benefit of teaching somebody in their own language and the effect of learning something new within the context of your culture

So, what should be the universal language and culture of the church? The answer in my opinion is:

Jesus Christ and His power of redemption.

Anybody can be saved by Him; no other message will help our lost humanity.

The universal culture of church membership should be to *'take up your cross and follow Christ'*.

When we all follow Christ, nobody will be lost because we are tempted to idolise people.

You can lose yourself while following a church denomination or personality.

Jesus came to introduce us to the father God and at the appointed time He returned to heaven, but He left the holy spirit behind to be in charge of the Church on earth.

Therefore, all churches are to be connected to the Holy Spirit for guidance and to avoid that is to become an ordinary social gathering where teas and coffees are just served, and lives may not be transformed.

Paul said in (1 Corinthians 2:5)

' so that your faith might not rest in the wisdom of men but in the power of God'.

'A church is a group of Christians not necessarily the building where they worship. The christians should be people who worship God and live according to His will'

- Harry Clayson, Musselburgh.

'A church should be a place where everyone is accepted and loved' – Niyi Oludipe Edinburgh.

CHAPTER ONE

One lord One faith one baptism
We believe in one God,
the Father, the Almighty,
maker of heaven and earth,
of all that is, seen and unseen.
We believe in one Lord, Jesus Christ,
the only Son of God,
eternally begotten of the Father,
God from God, Light from Light,
true God from true God,
begotten, not made,
of one Being with the Father;
through him all things were made.
For us and for our salvation
he came down from heaven,
was incarnate of the Holy Spirit and the Virgin Mary
and became truly human.
For our sake he was crucified under Pontius Pilate;
he suffered death and was buried.
On the third day he rose again

in accordance with the Scriptures;
he ascended into heaven
and is seated at the right hand of the Father.
He will come again in glory to judge the living and the dead,
and his kingdom will have no end.
We believe in the Holy Spirit, the Lord, the giver of life,
who proceeds from the Father and the Son,
who with the Father and the Son is worshiped and
glorified,
who has spoken through the prophets.
We believe in one holy catholic and apostolic Church.
We acknowledge one baptism for the forgiveness of sins.
We look for the resurrection of the dead,
and the life of the world to come. Amen.
(The Nicene creed).

COMING OUT OF DARKNESS

Darkness is a partial or total absence of light, gloom, wickedness, or evil.

It stands for spiritual obscurity hopelessness, barrenness, death and confusion.

Darkness will never go away from us, but as a church – we have been called out of it.

Hence the name – church (the called out). When a person wants darkness to go away, there is an active role to play in moving towards the light or switching a light on.

Illumination and direction is the main function of the light for it gives vision.

The church is a source of illumination to every generation, it is ignorant for any - one to imagine or conclude that the church is powerless or no longer relevant.

The church is beyond the building, it is a spiritual edifice a global and universal people with a common Lord, Jesus Christ the only potentate.

Jesus said, *"while I am in the world, I am the light of the world"*.

Darkness hides or twists information it creates a wrong identity of a situation or person but

Light reveals what is hidden, it makes situations clearer and vision brighter.

Darkness will not go away voluntarily because the prince of darkness - Satan hides himself in crafty ways, he wants people to remain in darkness so he navigates and controls the actions and spirit hoping that being a member of the church will hide their identity so they can

wreak havoc in the body but God exposes such agents of darkness in dramatic and unexpected ways.

Darkness leads to confusion, despair, lack of direction and possible death.

The world is in gross darkness and it has been since the beginning confirmed in the book of Genesis, news of violent attacks are everywhere now and it threatens to overwhelm us but God shines His light through these circumstances because He is omnipresent and He can appear in any situation where people invite Him.

A man called Saul was on the road to Damascus, he was convinced that he must destroy the "people of the way" which meant the Christians and so he pursued this goal with zeal. Little did he realise that he was in darkness until the light came to him.

(Acts 9:3)

'Now as he went on his way, he approached Damascus and suddenly a light from heaven shone around him'.

Whenever and wherever God is, light comes because God

is light but if we don't come closer to Him, darkness will encroach on us.

In remote villages where electricity is not connected yet, darkness prevails over the inhabitants and their activities for most of the night and the only way to illuminate the night is to light a candle or a lamp which are limited in function and even dangerous to health but when the electricity is connected, the paradigm of the environment changes.

People appreciate each other's company more and have more confidence to walk and play at night times.

THE OLD REBELLION

Man has always rebelled against God, authority and established systems. It is an inherent trait of man to rebel, to challenge the status quo and try something different.

Christianity and the church is no exception to the old rebellion however, the spiritual nature of the church and the covenant foundation of Christianity makes all rebellious acts against it sinful. some may be forgiven, and others may not.

Rebellion in the church and among Christians have been known to involve a rise against leadership style, preferences or perceived administration flaws and this is deeply rooted in the spirit of antagonism.

Antagonism is the major weapon the devil uses against the church, long before we were born Satan has always been an antagonist of God's kingdom and His creation most especially mankind. He hates us with an evil passion and is envious of our relationship with God.

. . .

He is described as the accuser of the brethren; he challenged God and is still doing so in various ways and means.

Why do we encounter antagonism?

Antagonism is a targeted attack on our purpose and mission, it is an offshoot of the spirit of envy and jealousy, anybody that is prone to the green - eyed monster is capable of antagonism because they usually imagine that other people are enjoying life at their expense.

Antagonism is the neighbour of rebellion and most revolutions stem from it because somebody is not happy with someone or something.

Bitterness invokes rebellion and the bottom line is written in (James 4:1-2)

'What causes quarrels and what causes fights among you? Is it not this, that your passions are at war within you? You desire and do not have so you murder, you covet and cannot obtain so you fight and quarrel ...'

Poverty in the spirit leads to envy and bitterness because the envious person is embittered about an issue that seems unjust to them but in reality they usually have no reason to feel that way but when a man is possessed with the spirit of envy, he becomes another person. He may lose all forms of empirical reasoning and do away with logical explanation only to charge into situations driven by emotions and feelings.

To be poor in the spirit is considered blessed by Jesus Christ only when it drives us to seek the kingdom of heaven and not to attack others or covet what they have.

It has been said that covetousness comes to us naturally, but contentment must be learned. It happens to the most spiritual and religious of us. We all fall into this temptation.

Man is a covetous creature; the grass always looks greener on the other side. We forget that the green grass is being kept by somebody. Envy makes a man reject God's plan for him and he seeks another plan because it looks better in his view.

The only antidote to covetousness is genuine information about who or what we are coveting and we need to pray that our souls may be delivered from the journey to destruction because as long as we are in this world and we don't control our greed, Nothing will ever be enough.

(1st Timothy 6:6) records that

' *godliness with contentment is great gain for we brought nothing into this world and it is most certain we shall leave with nothing'.*

When covetousness lingers in a person's heart , antagonism is not far away.

Lack of contentment is rampart in our world today and it is seeping into the church, though it carries a subtle appearance and names for instance;

'I claim it' 'receive it' , 'shout your way to blessing'.

We are advised to claim Abrahamic blessing but how many are prepared to do what Abraham did?

He believed God against all hope. He was childless for many years and when he eventually got his dream son, God came again that he should sacrifice that same son.

Is God deliberate in making us suffer? Certainly not! The answer is to trust Him completely with our lives.

Trusting God is an attribute which every man who claims to believe in God should learn if they will walk with Him for a longer period because God has been known to be quiet at times and we may be deceived into thinking that He has forgotten us.

So, when our trust diminishes, He remains the same, Trust and obedience is the key to walking with God.

. . .

Is antagonism a natural trait?

Some personality traits may open us to antagonism especially if one has a tendency to argue or not very agreeable. It is not ideal to be a push- over or be silent all the time however, outspoken people could end up becoming or being perceived as an antagonist.

In truth, antagonism is beyond our speech or opinion, but a systematic calculated and targeted plan to bring somebody or a system down, moreover many people with quiet dispositions have been known to lead a terrible rebellion especially now with the advent of social media. You don't need to open your mouth before you start a serious riot or quarrel.

Just put the word out there and say somebody else said it. Before a thorough investigation is carried out a reputation would have been destroyed.

ACTIVE AND DORMANT ANTAGONISTS IN THE CHURCH.

Antagonism is everywhere, we are only shocked when it is displayed in the church because the church is a family and we are meant to agree and unite but on the contrary when some people begin to think differently from the leader and the common vision, antagonism will creep in because the vision has been separated . When the leaders can't agree on issues in the church and conflicts start, look no further, antagonism is lurking underneath it is just hidden under a nice layer of 'holy outlook or appearance' but through prayer and discernment, church leaders will be empowered by the holy- spirit to spot the antagonists and correct them or if need be expel them.

To discern antagonism is to expect it to start from unexpected sources and only through the power of prayer can church leaders quench the rise of antagonism.

. . .

WHY DIFFERENCES ABOUND!

Some people say there is 'disunity' in the church because of the constant immature display of fights, bickering and petty quarrels but I submit in my humble opinion that the body of Christ is one and in unity but while the physical representative on earth – the church has many differences which is highlighted by our earthly sensual desires, the spiritual body remains intact and that is the church which Jesus Christ is coming for. - A transformed church.

Our differences do not intimidate God, He likes variety but hates disorderliness.

I have concluded after careful observations and study of major Christian denominations around the world that our major areas of differences lie in doctrines and values while the only concept of Christ' death resurrection that we all believe and accept unite us in faith, every other thing seems to divide us.

For instance , one Christian group may believe in complete modest clothing for attending a worship service or meeting while another believes in casual dressing to church as they propagate being 'comfortable' in God's presence, the bible is clear about how to appear before God, we can dress comfortably without being provocative.

We believe that the angels are with us constantly and they shouldn't have to use their wings to cover their eyes because of what someone is wearing in 'church'.

. . .

Modern day church leaders may be sending out mixed messages in churches, we say 'come as you are' then when they do come as they are, we are tempted to recommend another kind of clothing for their bodies instead of their spirit. When they are clothed in the spirit by the 'word' it will affect the unpopular fashion show in churches. Some people may require our prayers and patience while others require a good shopping assistance from experienced Christians.

CHILL OUT AT CHURCH

This is an emerging culture and the tradition of a generation who says one thing and act in another way. We want to see God's power yet we trivialise His word and His service.

We show up in church when we want, and sacrifice is a foreign word to us. Commitment has nearly disappeared, and faithfulness is almost a strange idea to discuss. We talk more than we act and pretend to be more than we really are. Striving for post but missing out in prayer meetings.

We have adopted a 'chill out at church' attitude in church whereby we reserve all our unfinished business and discussions to the church.

Text messages are not replied on time because 'we will see in church'.

We don't chill out at our work, on sports ground even in hospitals when we are ill but when we arrive in church, we want to chill out.

Sunday morning becomes the day that we relax because we have been working hard all week'.

The question is who did you work for during the week?

What makes us think that God is our 'playmate', the bible describes Him as a 'fearful and jealous God'.

Our play - ground attitude to the service of God is

robbing us of knowing the true God who made all the universe.

He spoke to Moses when he was being sent to Pharaoh (Exodus 8 :1)

'and the Lord said to Moses, go to pharaoh and say to him, let my people go that they may serve me'.

FAITH AND OBEDIENCE – ABRAHAM AND SARAH

People talk about faith all the time and I get that we must live by faith but what is the place of obedience because our faith is meant to mature us to a point where God gives us instructions and we carry them out as if our lives depend on it and truly it does .

Obedience to any child of God must get to a stage where we pray that His kingdom come, and His will be done for every area of our lives. It may take a while but walking with God produces finer version of who we are.

Abraham and Sarah's name were changed because of the will of God and purpose for their lives. To have faith is to hear and so what God says even when it appears strange.

To ignore God is to open ourselves to fallacy fantasy and the facade of evil that is prevalent in our world.

Roberts Liardon wrote in his book ' sharpen your discernment '

'Many Christians have never even thought about developing their spiritual awareness of the person of the Holy Spirit of God, some look to the media or just books to find out what God is doing. You will never know God or understand the situations of life aside from the bible.

Within the word are the principles and the character of God once we learn it the word will help us to discern the situations we face.

'The word of God will label all situations and people'.

If we don't know the word of God as it is written in the bible and apply it accordingly by wisdom of the holy spirit , the changes in our world will floor us spiritually and confusion may reign in our lives even when we proclaim that we are christians.

THE SPIRITUAL NATURE OF THE CHURCH

I have met and spoken to a few people concerning their views of how they see the church and I have listened to some of their answers that range from the church being a place of worship to a community of loving friends.

In the words of Jesus Christ himself, I gathered that the church is a spiritual place similar to the garden of Eden, with angels being on guard.

In the book of revelation, the churches are described as the lampstands and they have angels.

In (Revelation 2:1) *To the angel of the church in Ephesus write, the words of him who holds the seven stars in his right hand , who walks among the seven golden lampstands'.*

The meaning of these verse is that Jesus the head of the church walks in the midst of the church so every member of the church needs to be aware of this and be sober and reverent in the church.

That is why we are admonished in psalms 100:4 to enter *'his gates with thanksgiving' and 'his courts with praise'.* For the mighty power and strength that He holds and yet he is a merciful God who shows compassion on us daily.

In the sermon on the mount, Jesus informed the crowds that the way to be blessed in the kingdom of God is to do the opposite of what the world is doing.

'Blessed are the poor in spirit for theirs is the kingdom of God'.
'Blessed are the meek for they shall inherit the earth'.

. . .

11

CHURCH DISPENSATIONS

Dispensationalism is the method of interpreting history that divides God's work and purposes toward mankind into different periods of time. While some people have chosen more or less numbers of dispensations to focus on, we shall look at seven of them in this book.

The first dispensation is called the Dispensation of Innocence. This dispensation covered the period of Adam and Eve in the Garden of Eden. In this dispensation God's commands were to replenish the earth with children, subdue the earth, have dominion over the animals, care for the garden, and abstain from eating the fruit from the tree of knowledge of good and evil. God warned of the punishment of physical and spiritual death for disobedience.

This dispensation was short-lived and was brought to an end by Adam and Eve's disobedience in eating the forbidden fruit and their expulsion from the garden.

The second dispensation is called the Dispensation of Conscience, and it lasted about 1,656 years from the time of Adam and Eve's eviction from the garden until the flood . This dispensation demonstrates what mankind will do if left to his own will and conscience, which have been tainted by the inherited sin nature. The five major aspects of this dispensation are: a curse on the serpent, a change in womanhood and childbearing, a curse on nature, the imposing of difficult work on mankind to produce food, and the promise of Christ as the seed who will bruise the serpent's head (Satan).

. . .

The third dispensation is the Dispensation of <u>Human Government</u>, God had destroyed life on earth with a flood, saving just one family to restart the human race. God made the following promises and commands to Noah and his family:

1. God will not curse the earth again.
2. Noah and family are to replenish the earth with people.
3. They shall have dominion over the animal creation.
4. They are allowed to eat meat.
5. The law of capital punishment is established.
6. There never will be another worldwide flood.
7. The sign of God's promise will be the rainbow.

Noah's descendants did not scatter and fill the earth as God had commanded, thus failing in their responsibility in this dispensation. About 325 years after the flood, the earth's inhabitants began building a tower, a great monument to their solidarity and pride. God brought the construction to a halt, creating different languages and enforcing His command to fill the earth. The result was the rise of different nations and cultures. From that point on, human governments have been a reality.

The fourth dispensation, called the <u>Dispensation of Promise</u>, started with the call of Abraham, continued through the lives of the patriarchs, and ended with the Exodus of the Jewish people from Egypt, a period of about 430 years. During this dispensation God developed a great nation that He had chosen as His people.

The basic promise during the Dispensation of Promise was the Abrahamic Covenant. Here are some of the key points of that unconditional covenant:

1. From Abraham would come a great nation that God would bless with natural and spiritual prosperity.
2. God would make Abraham's name great.
3. God would bless those that blessed Abraham's descendants and curse those that cursed them.
4. In Abraham all the families of the earth will be blessed. This is fulfilled in Jesus Christ and His work of salvation.
5. The sign of the covenant is circumcision.
6. This covenant, which was repeated to Isaac and Jacob, is confined to the Hebrew people and the 12 tribes of Israel.

The fifth dispensation is called the Dispensation of Law. It lasted almost 1,500 years, from the Exodus until it was suspended after Jesus Christ's death. This dispensation will continue during the Millennium, with some modifications. During the Dispensation of Law, God dealt specifically with the Jewish nation through the Mosaic Covenant, or the Law, found. The dispensation involved temple worship directed by priests, with further direction spoken through God's mouthpieces, the prophets. Eventually, due to the people's disobedience to the covenant, the tribes of Israel lost the Promised Land and were subjected to bondage.

The sixth dispensation, the one in which we now live is the Dispensation of Grace. It began with the New Covenant in Christ's blood This "Age of Grace" or "Church Age" starts with the coming of the Spirit on the Day of Pentecost and ends with the Rapture of the church.

This dispensation is worldwide and includes both Jews and Gentiles. Man's responsibility during the Dispensation of Grace is to believe in Jesus, the Son of God. In this dispensation the Holy Spirit indwells believers as the Comforter. This dispensation has lasted for almost 2,000 years, and no one knows when it will end.

We do know that it will end with the Rapture of all born-again believers from the earth to go to heaven with Christ. Following the Rapture will be the judgments of God lasting for seven years.

The seventh dispensation is called the Millennial Kingdom of Christ and will last for 1,000 years as Christ Himself rules on earth. This Kingdom will fulfill the prophecy to the Jewish nation that Christ will return and be their King. The only people allowed to enter the Kingdom are the born-again believers from the Age of Grace and righteous survivors of the seven years of tribulation. No unsaved person is allowed access into this kingdom. Satan is bound during the 1,000 years. This period ends with the final judgment. The old world is destroyed by fire, and the New Heaven and New Earth will begin.

(adapted from Gotquestion.org).

CHAPTER TWO

'Nothing is as free as God's grace but nothing is as misused as that same grace'.

ABUSING GRACE AND LOVE

Grace is the ability to extend kindness to the unworthy and that's what God does to us every day and we ought also to receive others by grace. It is God's favour shown to us so when we show favour towards others, we are extending our grace to them but when the door is slammed in the face of our grace how do we respond?

Since grace is meant to be free, no man should owe another in terms of grace. It comes from God directly to us and flows to other humans as benevolence and kindness.

When a man receives grace, kindness becomes automatic, that is why the ten virgins in Matthew 25 took lamps but prepared at different levels to one another. Grace keeps us prepared as we look towards the return of the master Jesus Christ because no man knows the day and hour when He will return.

Grace is what keeps us in God and moves us forward everyday as we await the perfection of our salvation.

Such grace was bestowed on the prodigal son – who is a rather pitiable symbol of the modern - day church that has received a lot of revival and prophecies but is just sitting around wasting time and squandering her wealth on frivolities instead of reaching out to lost souls.

The modern- day church goers seem to view church attendance as one of those things and there is a lot of looseness to the spirit of God but looking through the bible, evidence shows that attending the church is a major way of receiving healing and daily victory.

' they go from strength to strength each of them as they appear in Zion.

The church is not an ordinary place whereby we commute to as we intend or prefer. It is the assembly of heavenly beings the presence of spiritual witnesses, angels ministering spirits and the appearance of the trinity.

As the fear of God is so should anybody who attends church should hold the essence of God in His temple. God dwells in churches by His spirit and His angels guards the perimeter always.

THE SHUNAMITE SPIRIT – TO LOVE AND TO SERVE

. . .

Dedication is disappearing fast from our generation, replaced by the expectation to get anything we desire by any means available without thinking of the consequences.

Acts of service and sacrifice is not popular as we receive messages of instant gratification everywhere we turn to but for the church or the christian, sacrifice and service is the only way to live fully..

Jesus paid with His life to redeem mankind and also the church.

One of the many acts of service and sacrifice is prayer.

To reach out to God in surrender and helplessness calling on Him to intervene in human interactions.

Prayer opens our hearts, it is an act of uttermost humility and dependence on God .

The shunammite woman saw an opportunity to serve and she took it which resulted in her receiving a miracle.

(2^{Kings} 4:8)

' one day Elisha went to Shunem, where a wealthy woman lived who urged him to eat some food, so whenever he passed that way he would turn in there to eat food'.

Every christian should adopt a Shunem spirit, whereby we can be a place where the world can turn to for food.

Many examples fill the bible and our generation of people who just wanted to serve but became pillars of history.

The way to God's heart is service and it never fails to move God into action.

When God speaks there is a purpose to His words and a reason to His voice.

We belong to God so we are meant to serve Him anywhere we find ourselves in this world

Change of location doesn't change who your parents are We belong to God anywhere anytime.

. . .

THE EMERGENCE OF SELFISM

Wikipedia describes Selfism as any philosophy theory doctrine religion or tendency that upholds explicitly selfish principles as being desirable .

Selfism to cut a long history short is "the gospel according to saint ME.

Whenever our attention shifts to ourselves instead of the common good the end result is selfism. It is not a word that most people want to be described with but sadly selfishness and self centeredness is at the root of most crisis in homes, workplaces and our churches.

We must have what we want or all hell will break loose, the pastor must be transferred, elders must be suspended or I move on to another church and recycling continues.

Most people proclaim their goodness at every opportunity but when the chips are down, we all choose what works for us best sometimes at the expense of others.

Personally, I have observed selfism in myself and others and discovered that the way you arrange your life can make it a bridge or a wall.

A bridge will lead people somewhere other than where they are but a wall will stop them.

A life of selfism is a life lived as a wall. Nobody passes through you.

. . .

Our world will only be touched and outreach can only be done and be productive by those who are willing to abandon self and move towards connecting with others even when it hurts to do so sometimes.

In a recent church attendance poll in the UK it was discovered that 72% of people that attended a church for the first time came because someone invited them.

Jesus Christ left His glory in heaven to be born into this earth of shame and disgrace, He was not even born or raised in a palace for consolation but in a manger.

Even the wise men went to seek him in the palace because that is where kings live naturally but the king of kings chose another location to be born because the palace is not accessible to all; He came for all and whosoever. He lived a life of bridge. His ideologies, proverbs, sayings and commandments were focused on helping others and doing the will of God, when temptation came in the garden of gethsemane and He wanted to refocus the attention to Himself, He caught Himself on time and said ' not my will lord but thine will be done'

LOSS OF SHARP DISCERNMENT

One of the major issues in the church of today in my opinion is the loss of sharp spiritual discernment which means to identify when God is no longer in the room or allowed to operate fully.

Discernment is not only to detect evil but to uncover the good in every circumstance.

. . .

Roberts Liardon wrote in his book 'sharpen your discernment' and I quote

Develop your spiritual relationship just like you would develop a natural one. A divine and intimate relationship begins so easily, just talk to God. Learn to live thankfully for everything you have and everything God continues to give. Hunger for God creates a purpose and a cause within you, that kind of godly purpose causes you to be swift and discerning.

The government of God is in the spirit realm not the political as a political leader is strong in his nation so should we be strong in the spiritual realm ..

Sadly the church is filled with people who have no idea how to rule in the spirit realm, most of us do our battles in the flesh even though the scriptures has it written that our battle is not against flesh and blood '.

We bring every matter of the church into the natural realm and we seem to have forgotten that our greatest weapon is prayer.

SPIRITUAL GIFTS IN THE CHURCH.

It is often expected that the church is operating in the power of God to heal and deliver save souls and release the captives.

All these demands on the power of God are valid but He needs human beings to cooperate with him.

When anybody accepts Christ and they are saved they are baptised into the spiritual body of Christ and so it is expected that they grow

. . .

1 Peter 2:2 advises that

'As newborn babes desire ye the sincere milk of the word that ye may grow thereby'.

What this means is that spiritual growth is the ultimate purpose of everybody in church and when this is lacking there will be organised chaos and random acts of rebellion.

Jesus Christ admonished His disciples by saying they need to grow in love and multiply so that the world may know that they belong to the father. He also warned them of the danger of not growing which is a cut -down by the 'father'.

The church is God's business and He has invested His best into the church in the person of our Lord Jesus Christ who is alive forever more and is over the church.

When a business owner is alive, the business will receive attention as it should therefore, the church on earth receives attention form the heavenly assembly whose leader is Jesus Christ.

OFFENCE

It has been defined as an 'annoyance or resentment brought about by a perceived insult to or disregard for oneself.

The church of today is filled with people who have a high sense of entitlement so even normal human interaction can be perceived as offensive because of high level of pride. Even if you offer a 'warm' tea instead of a 'hot' tea is likely to create offence for those who are prepared for it.

We come to church expecting a red-carpet welcome. Mixed messages have damaged us because some churches welcome people with teas and coffees and while this is a good and welcoming concept it may present the message of salvation in a familiar and casual way.

The regular kind of offences perceived in churches are textbook excuses made to depart from church leaving the regular worshippers to wonder if they did something wrong, some may include ; ' I don't feel loved, the service was too long, I feel bad when they read the bible. e.t.c.

Sin is bad and real. Teas and coffees will not wash it away but a true and genuine cry for the help of God who can save to the uttermost from the damnation of hell.

'Wherefore he is able also to save them to the uttermost that come unto God by him, seeing he ever liveth to make inter-cession for them'.- Hebrews 7:25

To avoid offence, our churches would fare better by not creating a near perfect atmosphere in the church, no group is perfect. Jesus should be introduced to church visitors when they come in and transformation should be discussed with them. They should be prayed for to have the road to Damascus experience when they come to us.

Jesus can not be served on a tray of croissants but the holy spirit is the person that introduces Him to everyone that comes with a hungry heart and not just a hungry tummy.

UNBIBLED GENERATION- we have a generation of disbe-lievers in church and open sinners from outside who are not engaging with the Bible maybe because they don't understand it or they are oblivious to its power. We basically lack the conversion experience and the transforming power and have replaced it with gimmicks and time wasting games.

What we need is transformation, Jesus Christ spoke to His disciples and they were transformed from ordinary men to fishers of men and eventually apostles of our great faith. He knew that nobody can access the secret of God until they are transformed. The transformer is God and the agent of transformation is the word of God by the holy spirit .

The early church was built on transformation and it involves waiting 'on God'

Luke 24:49 "And now I will send the Holy Spirit, just as my Father promised. But stay here in the city until the Holy Spirit comes and fills you with power from heaven."

Transformation affects every area of our lives .

For some it may mean maturity in spiritual things or service. Accepting persecution growing inward and outward.

TO JOIN A CHURCH.

When it's time to join a church, I often hear people say am still 'looking around' .

You can't just look around without pray around because unless you are directed to a church by the spirit of God and you stay through prayers and commitment you can start looking again very soon. Every church is filled with imperfect people that are living their lives before a perfect God.

When you join a new church for the first time, you are welcome with excitement but after a few months you are expected to put your back to the work of the lord without which your roots may not dig deeper and it may be easier for you to move along to the next church.

Every congregation has a special DNA and unless you become like them in purpose and value you may stick out as a sore thumb or most commonly become a thorn in their flesh.

Some churches have adopted the plan to become all things to all men and they are slowly becoming a community centre.

Teaching people what they want to hear so they don't get angry and leave the church.

The truth of the word of God has not been written for the pleasantness of the human soul.

Our soul needs to be cleansed, Jesus Christ said 'Ye are clean by the word I spake unto you'.

The church was formed by 'the word' and it must be sustained by 'the word'

'When I was a child I spoke like a child '

CHAPTER THREE

IS GOD STILL IN THE HEARTS OF OUR YOUTHS?

Many years ago author Paul Scherer alerted us to this down-
ward slide. Referring to the volatile exchanges between the
Church and its detractors he said:

"One by one the generation that refused to be bound by
the Pope, and refused to be bound by the church, decided in
an ecstasy of freedom that they would not be bound by
anything, not by the Bible, not by conscience, not by God
Himself. From believing too much that never did have to be
believed, they took to believing so little that for countless
thousands of human existence and the world itself no longer
seemed to make any sense. Poets began talking about the
`wasteland,' with ghostly lives,' as Stephen Spender put it,
`moving among fragmentary ruins which have lost their
significance.' Nothingness became a subject of conversation,
nihilism a motive, frustration and despair a theme for novel-
ists and dramatists, and the `edge of the abyss' as much of a
nautical term among the intelligentsia as it was for explorers

in the days of Columbus!" (Paul Scherer, <u>The Word God Sent</u>, Harper & Row, 1965, p. 11).

God fills everything according to (Acts 17:28) so who can escape Him?

No man can escape God because His spirit always longs for man, though man has done everything possible to discredit His existence and appearance both in personal lives and in the church.

The mass exodus from church that we experience is a revolution against the existence and clarity of God and His influence in our lives.

Will the church ever go into extinction?

Most certainly not, in almost every decade a new church is usually born albeit with a new, unusual or unfamiliar style of worship and culture that may confuse the preceding church culture and stiff opposition may arise however considering the fact that the main aim of every Christian church is to gather and worship God, over time the new church becomes accepted and celebrated.

The core of Christianity is the worship of God and propagation of the salvation that Jesus Christ brought to mankind, most modern arguments and ancient war is predominantly concerned with the eradication of this core belief and freedom that man stands to receive in Jesus Christ.

(Isaiah 43: 19-21) ESV

'Behold I am doing a new thing; now it springs forth, do you not perceive it?

I will make a way in the wilderness and rivers in the desert.

The wild beasts will honour me, the jackals and ostriches

For I give water in the wilderness, rivers in the desert to give drink to my chosen people the people whom I formed for myself that they might declare my praise'.

CHAPTER FOUR

BEYOND THE PULPIT

'Fear not little ones, it is my father's good pleasure to give you the kingdom – Luke 12:32)

When Jesus Christ rose from the dead after His crucifixion He gave the commandment to the disciples to go into all the world and make disciples of all . No location was exempted! It is accurate to conclude that the followers of Jesus Christ are heeding the call as churches are set up in little corners of the world.

The Greek word for church denotes ' to call out of' into something.

It has been understood to mean a spiritual body or assembly of both living and dead Christians.

It is a convocation, a gathering and an agreed body of people who accepts that their main leader is Jesus Christ who gave a set of commandments when He was leaving the earth concerning the spread of the gospel and the gathering of people to themselves and to God.

We are told to find the lost, so we receive the assignment of a Shepherd and that is where pastors come in, there are many lost sheep in the world those who have lost their way due to the darkness of the world and they are stumbling about , heading for eternal destruction but when God calls pastors, the assignment to find the lost is given to them by divine calling.

Some modern churches declare that they don't have a pastor but just 'elders'. While this appeals to them and may make every -body feel good , in my opinion it is a 'user friendly approach' to church leadership style because according to the scriptures, a church should have someone that God has a conversation with about people's destiny and that person is called the pastor.

I find it very strange and unbiblical for a church not to have a pastor either by appointment of board or by independent commission.

A pastor under independent commission is a church started by a person single or married who gathers disciples after a period and they in turn begin to raise other followers.

A pastor appointed by board is usually paid by agreement and contract but it doesn't mean they are less effective in ministry.

Jesus Christ was not an elder.

He is the good shepherd and He

is the head of the church. He did not appoint elders to seek the lost, they are just to administer and oversee the church matters.

While some may have pastoral calling it is not entirely directed enough for the great commission especially when you have a group of elders, seeking the lost just seems to get pushed around the meeting room table.

The chief shepherd of the congregation is the pastor and he will appoint or approve elders to handle church assignments which may include seeking the lost but they need to have a sound reporting system so that seeking 'the lost' doesn't become seeking 'my lost'.

Most church split are the offspring off untrained and uncensored ' seeking the lost' pattern that is borne out greed and over- ambition to become a 'general overseer'.

There is no strategy to prevent church split because the heart of man is desperately searching for quick success and a big church is always a big temptation to those seeking to start a church for themselves.

The only thing I have observed and suggest that can assist the flock not to follow the ' stranger shepherd ' is for the pastor to speak the truth directly from the pulpit and allow congregants to know the dangers of hirelings and to lead them in fervent prayers against such actions in a timely way.

The main duties and calling of the pastor is to seek the lost both in the world and in the church and the assignment is directly given to them by Jesus Christ in (Luke 15:4-6)

'What man of you having an hundred sheep if he loses one of them does not leave the ninety and nine in the wilderness and go after which is lost until he finds it? And when he found it he lays it on his shoulders rejoicing. And when he comes home he calls together his friends and neighbours saying unto them rejoice with me for I have found my sheep which was lost'.

Jesus recognised that the world is full of people who are lost so He appoints those who are 'Shepherds' by nature and intention and He put them over the household called 'The church'

The church is also full of the lost because many people feel lost due to lack of spiritual direction.

Recently, God spoke to my heart while I was cleaning and informed me that while I clean physically the same way , He cleans people's lives spiritually because people are messy and they go to church with their mess. So I must be prepared to deal with mess.

He also said, the mess can't pay the cleaners' wages but the person who employs the cleaner.

The headship of the New Testament church is a pastor not even a prophet

The pastor may have prophetic gifts among other spiritual and natural gifts but the essential assignment is to 'pastor'

To guide, counsel protect and lead the flock to righteousness in Christ.

(Romans 16:5) *'Greet also the church in their house'.*

The beauty of the church is that it can start from almost anywhere because Jesus Himself confirmed this when He said where two or three are gathered in 'his name', He promised to be in their midst.

The best place for church to start is from the home so every Christian family is a branch of the global church.

THE CHURCH IS FULL OF TRAUMATISED PEOPLE

Trauma has been defined as

'The result of an overwhelming amount of stress that exceeds one's ability to cope, or integrate the emotions involved with that experience'- Wikipedia

Around 1 in 3 adults in England report having experienced at least one traumatic event.

Traumatic events can be defined as experiences that put either a person or someone close to them at risk of serious harm or death. These can include:

- road accidents
- violence/prolonged abuse
- natural disasters
- serious illnesses.

What happens when you experience a traumatic event?

When you experience a traumatic event, your body's defences take effect and create a stress response, which may make you feel a variety of physical symptoms, behave differently and experience more intense emotions.

This fight or flight response, where your body produces chemicals which prepare your body for an emergency can lead to symptoms such as:

- raised blood pressure
- increased heart rate
- increased sweating
- reduced stomach activity (loss of appetite).

This is normal, as it's your body's evolutionary way of responding to an emergency, making it easier for you to fight or run away.

Directly after the event people may also experience shock and denial. This can give way over several hours or days to a range of other feelings such as sadness, anger and guilt. Many people feel better and recover gradually.

However, if these feelings persist, they can lead to more serious mental health problems such as post-traumatic stress disorder (PTSD) and depression.

Post-traumatic stress disorder (PTSD)

People experiencing PTSD can feel anxious for years after the trauma, whether or not they were physically injured.

Common symptoms of PTSD include re-experiencing the event in nightmares or flashbacks, avoiding things or places associated with the event, panic attacks, sleep disturbance and poor concentration. Depression, emotional numbing, drug or alcohol misuse and anger are also common.

The most effective therapeutic approach for long-term, severe PTSD appears to be talking treatments with a clinical psychologist, in which the person with PTSD is encouraged to talk through their experiences in detail. This may involve behavioural or cognitive therapeutic approaches.

Antidepressants may also be prescribed to relieve the depression which people who have survived trauma often experience at the same time.

Depression

Depression is different from feeling down or sad. Someone experiencing depression will experience intense emotions of anxiety, hopelessness, negativity and helplessness, and the feelings stay with them instead of going away.

Talking therapies such as cognitive behavioural therapy (CBT) and some forms of counselling and psychotherapy work well for depression. Antidepressants may also be recommended, either on their own or in combination with talking therapies.

Find out more about depression

What to do after experiencing a traumatic event

Turn to others for support

It can be difficult to talk to close family or friends after a traumatic event. You may not want to cause them any distress or may simply want some space to process it all. However, it is important to be around other people when you feel able to, as they can help with your recovery and wellbeing. You do not have to talk to them about the experience. If you don't have anyone close by to talk to, you can contact one of the organisations below, who will be able to offer further help.

Look after yourself

It is important to look after your health and wellbeing. This can include taking a break or some time away to deal with your experience. You should also try and keep a healthy diet and stay away from drugs and alcohol, which can exacerbate the problem.

Seek professional help

If you are experiencing symptoms that are affecting your day to day life, it is important to get professional help as soon as possible so you can begin to get better.

- www.mentalhealth.org.uk

RETURNING TO HEALING THROUGH THE BIBLE

There is healing for any kind of human trauma especially if we engage with help.

My personal experience has taught me that human beings are resilient and healing is always available. I personally seek consolation in music and reading (bibliotherapy)

I lost my dad and brother within 10 years of each other. I still cry when I remember them but by faith and reading the scriptures believing what God said is true of those that pass away that we shall meet them again in heaven that gives hope.

It is hopeful to expect that we shall see again, however the experience has helped me to care for those who lose relatives especially when young people die.

The bible regulates behaviour and emotions because it can speak to the darkest soul and bring it to the light. The word of God is light. (Psalms 107:20)

'He sent forth His word and healed them, He delivered them from their distresses'

'Scripture engagement means more than merely reading the Bible's words. According to Paul Caminiti, senior director of mobilization with the Institute for Bible Reading, Scripture engagement is about *immersing* ourselves in the Bible. We were meant to bathe in the Word, to soak in it. He says many people are told to just "pray and read their Bible." We naively expect people to read their Bibles successfully without direction or guidance. The result, says Caminiti, is that people read the Bible in fragments, out of context, and in isolation. Caminiti suggests that the best way to reverse this shallow engagement is to teach people to read Scripture in larger portions, within its original context, and together in community.

Phil Collins, professor of Christian Educational Ministries at Taylor University, describes Scripture engagement as a process of marinating in and mulling over Scripture in a way that leads to transformative encounters with God. "It's not for information or guilt or pride," he says, "but to meet and know God. It is *relational*." Collins says that this kind of engagement leads us to delight in God and his ways (Psalm 119).

How Can We Facilitate This Kind of Deeper Engagement?

First, we need to help people focus less on *what* and more on *who*. New Testament scholar Scot McKnight teaches that the goal of reading the Bible is not to know our Bible; it is to know the God of the Bible. We must have the proper end in sight: not more information, but a deeper relationship with God.

'Second, we must read the Bible on the Bible's terms, not our own. We do not stand over Scripture and interpret it. Instead, we place ourselves under Scripture and let it interpret us. The Bible has authority over our lives, not the other way around'.

Third, we must help people see the book as a narrative compilation and not a reference manual for life. It is a story in which we participate. Glenn Paauw, author of *Saving the Bible from Ourselves*, says that even when people have access to a well-translated Bible they don't necessarily engage it well. Snacking on little bits of Scripture is not what God intended. If people see it simply as a spiritual reference manual, says Paauw, it will never inspire them to engage with joy, excitement, and anticipation. But if we help people see the Bible as a grand story in which God invites us to participate, it can inspire and transform.

WHEN PEOPLE LEAVE A CHURCH NOT 'THE CHURCH'

Some misconceptions about membership that I have encountered in my Christian walk is that most people assume that the church is just like any ordinary place so they can treat their entry and exit with less care. Some even become entitled and imagine that God or the pastor is owing them some form of gratitude for the services they render in the church.

They fail to recognise the price that Jesus paid for their soul and no amount of service or volunteering can ever match that sacrifice. I am not advocating for lack of appreciation or pushing people to do what they are not willing to do in church but whatever anybody wants to do.

Based on our earlier definition of church any Christian who attend church should be prepared to do three things :

Worship God only

Serve the church with a focus on God.

Pray for people with a heart for God.

. . .

Anything in church done out of these three motives is likely to invite chaos and confusion because our human heart is desperately in need of supernatural surgery.

People have expectations when they walk into a church and I have encountered a few from talking to people in churches and some of them are:

'The pastor should come and greet me when I arrive'

'The pastor's wife should smile at me'

'I should be made welcome after all I pay my tithe'.

'I must be loved despite what I do or how I behave God is love'.

None of these human expectations and desires is sustainable by any church on earth, they may be practised at an early stage of the church but as the church grows some of them will become almost impossible to fulfil or unmanageable entirely.

For most Christians, we have been badly socialised by the wrong gospel and the best way to be delivered is to understand and practice the following :

Give love unconditionally

Show love, don't demand it

Whatever you sow you will reap.

People come and go—that's the nature of life in general.

However, leaving a church isn't the same as changing jobs or deciding to move to another city.

A church is *family*. We structure it that way for a biblical reason.

We are one body with many parts , brothers and sisters, the bride of Christ, all images of intimate, family relationships with strong emotional connections that run deep.

You *know* these people. These people know you.

So, when your spiritual family wants to part ways, it hurts knowing the relationship *is* going to fundamentally change.

It's hard enough when you truly love them and they're called to another ministry or feel the Lord is moving them toward another season apart from you.

It's much worse when they harm you, sow discord, backbite, attack, and take people with them in their anger, bitterness, and rebellion.

When ministry relationships break down and it's time to part ways, you will find two types of departure: 'went,' and 'sent.' And each of them must be handled differently.

A case for love and unity in the church

Love is not a prayer point it is an action taken against or towards somebody to preserve their dignity.

Unity will not come by prayer it comes by mutual respect among people that work or live together irrespective of age or position.

Jesus prayed that the disciples may be one as Him and His father are one but if God keeps breaking His promise and forgets to raise Jesus Christ from the dead because 'something came up' or if Jesus did not humble himself and wanted the same position the devil desired am sure the trinity will not be in unity. The name of the godhead stands for agreement so if we want to be like God, agreeable ness must be our sole aim.

We may not like one another's viewpoint but we must work on our agreeableness.

Many people are so disagreeable towards others in the church and they are seeking and praying for unity.

Agreeableness is a personality trait manifesting itself in individual behavioural characteristics that are perceived as kind, sympathetic, cooperative and considerate.

Sometimes we blame our personality and disposition when things go wrong and we forget that certain things in life has no regard for personality and they include our worship and fear of God.

It is more of an attitude than expression no matter how quiet or exuberant a person is it doesn't remove the fact that God is greater than all.

CHAPTER FIVE

A little thought on repentance.

'To repent is to change one's attitude towards self towards sin towards God and towards Christ'

Repentance has been defined by dictionary.com as the activity of reviewing one's actions and feeling contrition or regret for past wrongs, which is accompanied by commitment to change for the better.

Other words to describe repentance are: Sorrow, regret, pricked conscience, remorse.

Repentance means to 'clean up your act'.

It may also stand for repair, reconciliation, restitution.

It is the admission of faults, acknowledgement of wrong - doing and taking proper precautions or seeking help to ensure that similar situations don't arise in the future.

Repentance is a definite prerequisite for salvation.

We recognise that salvation is a gift from God, but it came at a price and received by grace

(Ephesians 2:8)

'For by grace you have been saved through faith and this is not your own doing, it is the gift of God'.

Does repentance lead to salvation or will salvation give repentance?

Shall we compare it to a hen/egg and egg/hen situation. Neither can exist without the other.

A repentant man shall be saved and a saved man need to be repentant always for His heart not to stray from the commandment of God.

It is assumed that man can repent by his own strength but the moral evidence and the constant struggle and failure to attain a godly life in our world today is pointing to the fact that repentance like grace and faith is a gift of God to our heart which has great capacity to cling to evil.

(Proverbs 4:23)

'keep your heart with all vigilance, for from it flows the springs of life'.

No man can wilfully repent. It is not in us. It is the divine grace of God that pulls the strings of our sinful hearts. We are incapable of repenting of our own volition so the law of God is good for us to feed on.

The word of God has enough power in it to change our hearts, the constant reading and meditating on the scriptures tilts us towards godly sorrow and repentance.

Bible reading is very paramount to our constant dose of repentance without which our lust for the world will increase and we could be entangled in matters that will kill our conscience towards God.

Our most noble plan will be destroyed by the pull of the world if we keep away from reading the word of God.

(Joshua 1:8) *'This book of the law shall not depart out of your mouth'..*

Repentance is like surrender, it is a bridge to the future. an unrepentant soul is stuck in the past and will insist on having his own way by revenge or getting even.

An unrepentant soul forgets that he or she was cleansed from sin and a saviour died because of us.

Repentance, then, is the posture that leads us to pray in a similar fashion to that of the tax-collector in the lessons taught by Jesus Christ , *"God, be merciful to me, a sinner" (Luke 18:13b). The repentant heart can boldly call himself ' a sinner'.*

'A repentant soul is willing to be reproved and corrected, is not hasty to judge others, neither is it prideful.

Repentance kills pride: the more we learn God's laws and standards, the more we learn that we are incapable of saving ourselves or redeem our souls by our power'. (desiring-god.org)

Repentance against old and hardened sin:

some habits and attitudes have become so old and customary that we have stopped seeing them as sins e.g prayerlessness, lateness to the service of God, selfishness, not caring for others, individualism, regarding oneself above others, to mention a few.

The unrepentant soul use common clichés and phrases that goes thus:

'God understands'
'Nobody is perfect'
'God looks at the heart'
'God will help us '

. . .

Repentance as an open sinner and a false saint.

Many regard the drunkard by the road side as the only person in need of repentance and so we despise them and hope that God will save their souls from hell but there hope for all men according to (1John 2:2) to suggest that we all need to be saved from constant darkness that threatens to overshadow our heart.

'He is the propitiation for our sins and not for ours only but for the sins of the whole world'.

We need a saviour that must be kept close to our hearts in prayer so that we may not be contaminated and consumed by the sinfulness of the world.

We need to confess our transgressions regularly in order to purge ourselves of pride and deceitfulness of riches and security.

This is not the same as the regular confessional practised by religious orders based on their doctrines or ritual but an admission that without the saving power of Christ, we shall all be doomed to hell.

It is the stirring of the conscience towards godly actions.

This should lead us continually to the cross for our daily dose of grace. If we could pray for more faith, why not ask for more mercy and a heart that leans towards God.

(Proverbs 4:23) warns us :
'Above all else, guard your heart,
for everything you do flows from it.
Keep your mouth free of perversity;
keep corrupt talk far from your lips.
Let your eyes look straight ahead;
fix your gaze directly before you..
The heart can travel faster than we imagine, inside it

contains our life nuggets, insights, our next move whether good or bad.

This is where true repentance takes place. You don't need a witness or CCTV, your heart will stand as a judge if you have truly repented.

God will not only judge our physical actions but our hearts' intents and motives will be judged too.

(Deuteronomy 6:5-6)

"And *thou shalt love the Lord thy God with all thine heart, and with all thy soul, and with all thy might and these words, which I command thee this day, shall be in thine heart.*"

Benefits of repentance

There is only one benefit to repentance and it goes beyond human acceptance or keeping up appearances, it is the rerouting of our eternal destination by a sovereign God simply put as 'Deliverance from hell'.

If there was no hell or heaven, why are we afraid of dying? Just a thought!

There is no separate hell for men or women nor a different hell for sinners and saints. some say that Jesus had delivered us from the destiny of hell handed down from our fathers but I submit that a hardened heart and a continual life of ungodliness can open the way to hell and this applies to both sinners and saints . Consider Judas Iscariot!.

Finally, God declares in(Isaiah 1:13-19) that obedience is the key to repentance and any man who wants to unlock his destiny must keep the key of obedience closer to his heart and holiness without which no man shall see the lord.

BREAKING THE POWER OF GOSSIP IN CHURCHES

. . .

'Don't pass on malicious gossip.

Don't link up with a wicked person and give corrupt testimony. Don't go along with the crowd in doing evil and don't fudge your testimony in a case just to please the crowd. And just because someone is poor, don't show favouritism in a dispute'. (Exodus 23:1-3, the message version)

Gossip has been defined by dictionary.com as:

"a casual or unconstrained conversation or reports about other people, typically involving details which are not confirmed as true".

It is speaking about someone in a way that defames, dishonours or otherwise hurts their character. Sometimes it is subtle, like grumbling about someone, and other times it is loud, like ranting about someone. Further, sometimes the content of what is said is true, other times it is not.

Either way, the person hearing does not need to know the information, they don't benefit from it.

And, most times it is not actionable; they are not going to go and help the person, instead they are just going to tuck away the information for selfish use.

Gossip and its cousin slander, divisive speech and deceitful speech are roundly rebuked in the Scriptures Instead of cutting people down with verbal assassinations, we are to give words of life and grace.

Gossip is the negative issues that you discuss with people who can't help you.

It is a behavioural deficiency, a total lack of care for people's emotional welfare and a prideful sin that totally ignores the word of God that instructs us to care for one another.

An anonymous speaker said 'if *we had as much prayers in church as we have gossip, there will be a great revival'.*

A gossip usually feel they are somehow better than who they are talking about, forgetting that every man has their own failings, no matter how well - meaning if the information is not verified by the person it pertains to, it should not be received, believed, shared or acted on.

The motive of gossip is to slander and degrade somebody, a malicious intention to reduce somebody's influence or popularity, gossip destroys relationships, families , church systems and businesses.

In these days of social media people's reputation can be destroyed in an instant because gossip is never harmless, social media is the biggest form of gossip, nothing is ever checked out before people swallow it and share on other platforms.

Many are confused in today's world due to unverified and unchecked information received online and without any doubt gossip is the weapon of those who are weak and idle, regardless of the reasons, loose talk hurts,

Some people nearly take their own lives because of malicious comments passed around about them. victims of the gossip first of all feel embarrassed that their problems are now public, even strong and mature Christians deal with serious shortcomings daily so revealing private details of their struggles can harm others looking to them for strength.

Gossip is a problem because it is a habit rooted in sin according to (Matthew 7:12).

'*So whatever you wish that others do unto you, do same unto them*' this is the law and the prophets'.

Gossip violates our Lord's command to *'love one another'*

and often the gossip is untrue which adds to its sinfulness, gossip is simply wrong.

The spiritual dangers of gossip

1. Gossip kills your vision: A habitual gossip may find it difficult to receive a vision from the lord for the future because God cares for people and anybody that gossip about another human being is tearing them down so God can't work with a gossip. God's words are authentic and confirmed but a gossip tells stories that are not only false but remain unchecked.

The only element any gossip may enjoy from God is 'Grace' and an anonymous quote states that "You can't sow gossip and reap glory".

2. Gossip destroys prayer life: When you indulge in gossip you forget that man is made in the image of God so when it's time to pray God's spirit reveals to us what we really are and because a gossip doesn't usually like what they see in themselves when they pray, prayer time is often avoided.

3. The heart of a gossip is far from God because gossip is a manipulative and suggestive behaviour so the prayer of a gossip becomes an abomination to the lord.

4. Gossip compromises holiness: Holiness simply means obedience to God's direction without attempting to change God's plan. A gossip contradicts everything holiness stands for because they don't know the will of God nor His direction for their lives , they lack vision even if they receive a divine plan by a miracle they can't accept it nor act on it for fear of being rejected or talked about just like they do to others and this leads directly to disobedience and eventually loss of holiness.

5. Gossip breeds anxiety: Many things can cause anxiety in life but the greatest cause of it is gossip. Whether you are the subject of gossip or you are the one perpetrating the act

of gossip, it has a high chance of leading to anxiety and fear. People become uncomfortable in your presence or you in theirs. You can't look your friends in the eye when you meet them because you have destroyed them behind their backs. Nightmares are frequent in the lives of a gossip 6because the devil is the source of all gossip so he is not far from any one who indulges regularly in gossip.

6. Social connection becomes almost impossible because the gossip is unprepared for scenarios that may play out in public since they don't know who will turn up and start a conversation that will eventually confirm their words to be false or challenge them even if it the details happen to be true.

The role of church leaders in tackling gossip.

Church leaders have a spiritual and temporal responsibility and authority to bring gossip peddlers to light and pray for God's mercy on their soul.

Leaders must not indulge in gossip themselves but establish clear boundaries and systems about sharing of information .

Leaders must promote confidentiality among church officers and members.

A standard anti gossip policy needs to be developed and supported in the local churches through regular trainings and discussions.

A disciplinary procedure must be put in place to combat loose and uncontrolled tongues.

Churches should establish a clear communication channel between pastoral teams and church officers because due to lack of openness and trust, gossip may gain a foothold.

Antagonists should be identified, warned and prayed for.

They should be given a chance to repent but if they continue to create conflict in the church through gossip , they may be relieved of their leadership position in the church entirely because every church position is a position of influence and it should be used positively to encourage people to draw nearer to God and not the opposite.

Above all, prayers should be raised regularly against the spirit of gossip and the destructive power it exerts on people, asking the Lord to restore those whose lives have been affected by gossip and for the mercy of God upon the soul of those who perpetrate the act of gossip.

CHAPTER SIX

MAKING DISCIPLES

'If the church is not making disciples then all the cathedrals, clergy, missions, sermons even the bible are a waste of time'- Anonymous

Jesus said to His disciples *'follow me and I will make you fishers of men.'*

Are there still disciples in our world today? the answer is yes!

There are honest men and women who are seeking Jesus and his peace for their lives.

Discipleship was the main method of our Lord Jesus Christ when he lived on the earth though he spoke in parables to every other person he met but He 'explained' the meaning to the disciples much later in simple words so they could understand.

It wasn't a deliberate action to confuse those who are not disciples but because of intimacy and relationship Jesus had time for the disciples and He taught them what others could not wait to learn.

To learn about the God of the Christians and the church is to hang around Him in prayer reading the bible and reflecting on His words.

One major attribute that will lead to a victorious Christian life is to hear God's voice and obey it listening to His commands and putting them into action.

In (Luke 11:28) 'Jesus replied, *'But even more blessed are all who hear the word of God and put them in*to *practice'*.

Discipleship is friendship in disguise, an art of transforming an ordinary person into an extraordinary vanguard, totally loyal to the cause they are committed or assigned to.

For Christians, we are destined and designed to pay absolute allegiance to the cross of Christ and His victory so we are the people of the cross and of the way. Any life lived below this standard is deemed to be a carnal life, a divided and fragmented life.

Multitudes come for food but disciples come for knowledge and inheritance.

Some characteristics of a true disciple of the church derived from the bible are listed below

The loss of personal rights

Absolute love for God and others

A transformed and changing heart
Awakened conscience
Openness to the word of God
No hidden areas in character
Undivided in spirit soul and body
Always learning to know
Constantly giving cheerfully
Purposeful living

PRAYER! PRAYER!! PRAYER!!!

'If *you are looking for someone who rules the world, don't go seeking them in the palace, you will find them on their knees'- praying'.*

Prayer is talking to God, if you can talk you can pray. Just change your audience

Prayer is one of the basic Christian instructions, very simple yet complicated just like giving.

When it's time to pray, Jesus gave us a pattern and we have been following it for centuries.

This prayer patter focuses on the father who is in heaven but who gives us power on authority on earth so whatever we say on earth will be done in heaven and sent to us on earth.

Every church is filled with imperfect people, when you join as a new comer, you are welcome with excitement and greeted with love but after a few months it is biblical for everyone to be involved in the work of the kingdom and is assumed that you will do likewise for others after you.

. . .

Look around you, churches abound more than ever and we are almost tempted to visit or enlist the help of 'Compare the church.com' to seek where we should worship.

If that could help us but sadly no website can refer you to a great church and and give you lasting satisfaction there only your heart can make your church a fantastic church.

When your heart turns away from a church nothing that is done there will ever be enough.

Emergence of the internet church and E-membership.

There is nothing wrong with being an online worshipper but one thing is lacking and nobody has given me the clue. If everybody that was in the service that is broadcasted goes online to worship who will be in the video?

E - members will not cut the grass of our churches in nor sing worship on Sunday morning service while they record it , the church needs people with physical bodies there with physical body to serve and carry out duties.

If you love that man of God more than your pastor, are you prepared to relocate to be closer to his ministry? How many times do we pray for our churches and leaders before we raise concerns?

Every Christian should return to true humility and find a local church where the bible is being read openly and taught by the holy spirit and be prepared to discipled truthfully we all pray for the kingdom of God to come on earth.

In the words and prayer of Paul the apostle in (Acts 20:32)

'and now I commend you to God and to the word of His grace which is able to build you up and to give you the inheritance among all those who are sanctified'.

Printed in Great Britain
by Amazon

72748919R00040